THE JOY OF
MEDITATING

ALSO BY SALLE MERRILL REDFIELD

*The Celestine Meditations**

*Available from Time Warner AudioBooks

THE JOY OF MEDITATING

A BEGINNER'S GUIDE TO THE ART OF MEDITATION

SALLE MERRILL REDFIELD

With a Foreword by James Redfield

WARNER BOOKS

A Time Warner Company

A Time Warner Company

Printed in the United States of America
First Printing: November 1995
10 9 8 7 6 5 4 3 2

Library of Congress Cataloging-in-Publication Data

Redfield, Salle Merrill.
    The joy of meditating : a beginner's guide to the art of
meditation / Salle Merrill Redfield.
        p. cm.
    ISBN 0-446-67234-3
    1. Meditation.   I. Title.
BF637.M4R44   1995
158'.12—dc20

95-33297
CIP

Cover photo by Ted Grant
Cover design by Elaine Groh
Book design by Giorgetta Bell McRee

For my grandmothers,
Ruby Bray Merrill and Louise Caton Waller,
whom I have not been with in twenty years,
except in my meditations

ACKNOWLEDGMENTS

My heartfelt thanks to: Gail Nelson for her unconditional love and encouragement, Albert Clayton Gaulden, who intuited this book long before I understood its reality, and most of all to James, whose constant support has been invaluable.

ABOUT THE AUTHOR

SALLE MERRILL REDFIELD is the author and narrator of *The Celestine Meditations* and lectures on meditation internationally. She lives in Florida with her husband, James Redfield.

Meditate upon these things; give thyself wholly to them;
that thy profiting may appear to all.

FOREWORD

by James Redfield

We live in a time of accelerating change. The normal pace of life, at work, in our communities, at home, continues to increase almost beyond our ability to cope. For many of us life has become a series of rapid, even frenzied readjustments, as we try to keep up with and sort through all the options and demands of modern life, both for ourselves and our children.

At the same time, we live in a period of high expectations. We seem to sense inside that life isn't meant to be that way, that a mental approach exists in which we can more easily handle these responsibilities and sudden challenges. We want to be in the flow, "on top" of our day-to-day lives, instead of constantly feeling behind and scrambling to put out fires.

For an increasing number of people, meditation is becoming an important tool for altering how we handle stress and for improving our ability to enjoy the pace. I don't know that anyone can adequately convey just what spending minutes a day in calm mindfulness really does. Certainly the research has shown that meditation leads to the bodily changes associated with deep relaxation and removal of tension. But the perceptual changes are even more dramatic.

Because the mind is cleared of the meaningless chatter and redundancy, we seem to have more time and clarity to tend to the necessary details. Time seems to slow down, and we can not only stay ahead of the game but also stop to smell the symbolic flowers. We can reflect and be. Of course, all these changes are experiential. No one can actually comprehend such a shift until one has felt the effect personally. This book is for those who are ready to give it a try.

INTRODUCTION

I began to understand the full importance of meditation when I experienced a major life shift in 1989. During that year, I ended a seven-year marriage, sold my home, and moved away from my friends to another state. Due to the suddenness of this transition, I found myself living with a high degree of stress and anxiety. While I had meditated occasionally in the past, at this time I began to meditate on a daily basis.

After I moved, I learned of a group of people

in my new town who met weekly to explore the technique of meditation and prayer. The group was led by a very intuitive woman, who helped us relax, feel loved, and connect with a higher aspect of ourselves. My sense of well-being and comfort with the visualizations steadily increased. I looked forward to the weekly meditations and developed a bond with the members of the group.

Each week when we came together, we joined our meditative intention in order to help one another find solutions to current life questions. Some of the time we would gain insights immediately. Other times we would feel the residual effects of the peaceful evening later as we gained more clarity. No matter how we felt when the meditation began, we all felt a great sense of well-being when it ended.

Later, through a series of synchronistic events, I was asked to become this group's meditation leader, a preparation, as it turned out, for the meditations I would lead two years later for thousands, as my husband, James Redfield, and I traveled internationally, speaking about his book, *The Celestine Prophecy*. It also created the foundation for the meditations I recorded on the audiotape, *The Celestine Meditations*. It was during this book tour that I discovered just how popular meditative practice had become.

Once associated with Eastern religion or esoteric Western schools of thought, meditation is now understood as an extremely relaxing and beneficial "mental state," achievable by virtually anyone and on its way to becoming thoroughly established by science.

In Bill Moyers's now classic book and PBS special, *Healing and The Mind*, he explores the work and research of two nationally recognized leaders in the growing field of mind/body medicine: Jon Kabat-Zinn, Ph.D., and Dean Ornish, M.D.

Jon is founder and director of the Stress Reduction Clinic at the University of Massachusetts Medical Center and has developed an international reputation for using yoga and meditation to help medical patients suffering from chronic pain and stress-related conditions.

Jon's research through the Stress Reduction Clinic has shown the effectiveness of meditation in treating high blood pressure and anxiety—and, more important, in helping to prevent these problems. Positive effects have included heightened sensitivity, increased control of emotions, and expanded creative ability.

Dr. Ornish is an assistant clinical professor of medicine and the director of the Preventive Medicine Research Institute at the School of Medicine, University of California, San

Francisco. His research has demonstrated for the first time that coronary heart disease can be reversed by a disciplined program of improved diet, walking, and meditation—without the use of drugs or surgery.

In my daily life, the time I take to meditate is vital. When I slow down, become mindful, and remember to breathe deeply, I discover a sense of peace within myself. One of my favorite ways to meditate is by walking in a natural environment. I find that as I walk through wooded areas or along the ocean shore, I feel a deep connection to a Divine source. I also gain mental clarity and experience an increase in my creative flow.

With the benefits of meditation becoming more known in our society, many individuals are expressing interest in exploring meditative practice for themselves. The purpose of this book is to make this goal easier by introducing, in a very general way, meditation that emphasizes relaxation and the art of imagery and visualization.

The following four meditations are intended to be user-friendly and adaptable regardless of your life situation. They are organized sequentially, so it is important to practice the first meditation before moving on to the others. Each meditation will take about fifteen to twenty minutes to complete. Take time to fully visualize each thought.

I suggest that you keep this book by your bedside. Use it when you wish to relax and focus your thoughts. But remember, to be effective the meditations must be read with mindfulness and positive intention. Open your heart...and there you will find the joy of meditation.

FIRST MEDITATION

This meditation is designed to relax the muscles of the body and to reduce tension and anxiety. In the meditation experience, it is important that the body be relaxed before clearing the mind and opening ourselves to higher awareness. I recommend that you sit in a soft chair or stretch out on a bed or the floor. Very often, because of the stress most of us face in daily life, our bodies tend to develop tight, sore muscles at various locations.

The most common places are the back, neck,

and shoulders. If you have lower back problems, you may want to lie down and put a pillow under your knees in order to remove pressure in that location. During the meditation, you will be asked to tense your muscles slightly and then release. This "letting go" motion will enhance the relaxation process. You may find that as your body begins to relax you will need to adjust the way you are sitting or lying. This is normal. Also, make sure to keep your breath fluid and open throughout the entire meditation.

I believe that the best results are achieved when you play soft, instrumental music in the background. Music will help you further relax and focus your mind. As the meditation proceeds, you may find your mind wandering, or you may recall some worrisome moment from earlier in the day. This is a common occurrence.

Try to release these thoughts and realize you can return to them later.

Remember, this is a beginning meditation. There is no right or wrong way to do it. Just try to relax and follow the instructions as best you can. The more you practice the meditation, the easier it will become.

Meditation

As you begin the meditation, gently move the muscles of your body until you are situated in a comfortable position.

Allow your body to settle and sink into the chair, floor, or bed.

Now begin to notice your whole body in a mindful way. What areas of your body feel relaxed? Which feel tight?

Now notice your breathing pattern.

Feel your lungs expand and your chest

and stomach rise and fall as you breathe in and out.

Take a deep breath. Breathe in with your nose and out through your mouth. Release the air slowly.

Next, focus your awareness on your feet. How do they feel?

Tighten the muscles of your feet slightly for a couple of seconds…then release them.

Now focus on your calves.

Tense them slightly for a few seconds… and release.

And now your thighs. Tense and release them also.

If your legs remain tight, take a moment to tense and release them again.

Remember to adjust your body if you need to.

Next, notice how your hips, buttocks, and lower back feel.

See if you can release any tension you may be holding there.

Tighten the muscles in your buttocks for a second or two and release.

Now move your awareness to your stomach and intestinal region.

Many times there is anxiety stored in this part of the body because under stress there is a tendency to contract these muscles.

Consciously relax your stomach and intestines by taking a deep breath.

Now travel up to your chest.

Again feel your lungs expand and your chest open as you breathe in and out.

Focus next on the muscles of your back.

Move your back around slightly to help release any muscle tension.

To relax the muscles between your shoulder blades, arch your upper back slightly and push your shoulder blades together for a second or two and release them.

Another tendency you might have under stress is to keep your shoulders tensed up around your neck.

Make sure your shoulders are down and relaxed.

Notice how your neck feels after you have lowered your shoulders.

If the neck is a place where you feel tension, let's see if you can help diminish some of the discomfort.

Slowly and gently stretch the muscles of

your neck by turning your head as if you are looking from left to right.

It is important that your movements be slow and deliberate.

Be gentle with your neck and move it only as far as comfortable.

Now slowly move your head in a clockwise position and then in a counterclockwise position.

Feel your neck muscles begin to soften.

Now move your jaw around slightly and notice how it feels.

If it is sore and tight, clench your teeth and release once or twice.

Move your lower jaw from side to side and see if the clenching of your teeth helped loosen any tightness you might have felt in this area.

Take another deep breath and release slowly.

Now soften and relax your face by tensing and releasing your facial muscles.

Next, soften your forehead by squinting and then arching your eyebrows.

Try to fully relax your head.

Move your awareness to your arms and hands.

Squeeze your hands tightly for a moment and release them.

Tense and release the muscles of your arms.

Move your arms and hands around and then place them in a natural position.

Now count to ten slowly.

Feel your body becoming totally relaxed and limp, like a rag doll.

Take a moment to survey your body again.

If there are any parts of you that still need to relax, tighten that part of your body, and then release it.

Now take three deep breaths.

Again, breathe in deeply through your nose...and release the breath through your mouth.

Inhale again and hold it for four seconds before you breathe out.

Now the last breath: breathe in slowly, hold the breath for four seconds, and release.

Feel your body relax deeply because of the breaths.

Now feel as if a circle of healing light is surrounding you.

Feel your body absorb the light.

Use the light coming into your body to soften any part of you that needs more relaxation.

Breathe the light into your lungs.

Take a moment to feel the peace within your body and your connection to this loving, healing light.

Take one more deep breath before you end the meditation.

Release the image of the light, knowing it will remain with you.

When you are ready, move your body around slightly and open your eyes.

As you go about your day, remember to keep your shoulders down, breathe deeply, and visualize the healing light whenever you are feeling stressed and out of balance.

SECOND MEDITATION

The following meditation is designed to build on your ability to relax and quiet the mind as described by the first meditation. Once you have become accustomed to relaxing deeply, you will be ready to expand your awareness through the use of guided visualization.

The meditation will begin with a brief period of relaxation. Afterward, you will take a mental journey along a wooded pathway that leads to a crystal-clear stream. In this location you will sit down and immerse yourself in the surrounding beauty, visualizing the colors and forms. Imagine your surroundings as best you can. Trust the images you receive. If you don't see all the images fully or vividly at first, be patient with yourself. The more you practice the meditation, the easier it will be to visualize the scenes.

Meditation

Let's begin the meditation by taking a deep breath.

Slowly breathe in through in your nose and out through your mouth.

Make sure you are in a comfortable position and your back feels supported.

Now take a moment to survey your body and see how it feels.

Which parts of you have already begun to relax, and which parts are holding tension?

As in the first meditation, focus first upon your feet and see how they feel.

If they are tense, tighten them slightly and release them.

And now notice your legs. If they feel tight, gently squeeze and contract the muscles.

Remember to breathe as you relax your body.

Travel up your torso and back.

How does the upper part of your back feel?

Is the space between your shoulder blades tight or relaxed?

Move the shoulder blades around and see if that helps the muscles release.

If you are feeling any rigidity there, take a deep breath and use the breath to soften the muscles.

Breathe in and visualize the muscles loosening and letting go.

Now check your shoulders and make sure they are down and relaxed.

How is your neck feeling today?

Move your head slowly and gently, side to side, to help the neck muscles relax and soften.

Continue to focus relaxation on every part of your body.

Remember to squeeze and contract any tense muscles.

Now count to ten slowly.

Take three deep breaths.

Breathe in slowly through your nose and out your mouth.

Breathe in again and hold the breath

for four seconds, before you breathe out.

This is the last time: breathe in and hold...and release.

Notice your body again and adjust it if you need to.

Now prepare to take a mental journey down a wooded pathway to a peaceful stream.

Begin the journey by visualizing yourself standing in front of a gate.

Notice what the gate looks like. Is it plain and simple, or is it ornate and decorative?

Create the gate that is most appealing and inviting to you.

Realize that the gate is there to protect

the sacred places beyond. You are the only one who can go through, unless you decide to invite someone to join you.

Open the gate, walk through it, and close it behind you.

Begin to walk along the pathway that is in front of you.

Observe the tall trees, ferns, and green leafy plants that surround you.

What type of pathway are you walking on?

Is it a natural pathway or is it paved?

It is a beautiful summer day and the sun is shining.

There are fragrant wildflowers growing along the pathway. Stop for a moment and smell their perfume.

As you continue walking, feel as if you have left your everyday life behind for a short while.

Begin to hear the sounds of a stream flowing in the distance.

Step off the path onto the cool grass and walk toward the stream.

Take a moment to look around until you find a quiet and safe place to sit.

The place you choose may be on the grass, on a blanket, or on a rock. You may even choose to sit on a rock in the middle of the stream.

Find the place that is most appealing to you.

Now take a moment to sit quietly and study the environment.

There are beautiful trees around you with rich green leaves. You may see colorful wildflowers or a variety of plant life.

Look up the stream and notice how it flows over the gray and brown rocks. See the moss growing on some of the rocks.

Feel the cool shade provided by the overhanging trees.

See the reflection of the sun shimmering on the water.

Look at the stream and see if there are small fish swimming by. Observe their distinct shapes and colors.

Now listen to the sounds of the birds and crickets in the background.

The water flowing over the rocks bubbles and swirls in soothing rhythm.

Reach your hands into the stream and feel the coolness of the water. You may want to put your feet in the current.

Look into the water again and see if there is a pebble or stone on the streambed that attracts you.

Reach for it through the water and bring it to the surface.

Is the rock round and smooth or sharp and pointed? Take a moment to examine it.

When you are ready, return the stone to the stream.

Now lie back and gaze at the blue sky in the distance and at the white clouds that are floating by.

Feel the cool breeze on your body.

You are being nourished by the earth.

Realize that you are exactly where you are supposed to be.

Feel as if you are being watched over and cared for by a loving presence greater than yourself.

Take a moment to feel your connection to the beauty around you.

Feel a sense of love and peace sweep over your body, filling it with light.

Feel the light permeate the cells of your body and nourish it.

Breathe in deeply and feel at one with your environment and the Universe.

Breathe in again and connect with the beauty one last time.

When you are ready, prepare to leave this

sacred site, knowing you can return any-
time you want.

Take one last look at your surroundings.

Walk away from the stream and step
onto the path you followed earlier.

Know that a part of you has shifted
inside because of your experience.

As you make your way back, notice the
trees and wildflowers again.

See the gate in the distance.

When you reach the gate, open it slowly
and walk through.

Close it behind you and gradually prepare to end your meditation.

Move around slightly.

Take a deep breath before you continue
with your day.

THIRD MEDITATION

Like the last meditation, this meditation builds on the descriptions of the previous meditations.

It begins with relaxing your body and then again takes you on a journey down a wooded path to a stream, reviewing the images and sense of beauty experienced before.

After a brief time, you will continue along the pathway until you reach a majestic, freshwater lake. Here you will reach out and explore the experience of love. The purpose of this meditation is to explore a deeper experience of the Divine.

For the next fifteen to twenty minutes relax your body and enjoy your adventure.

Meditation

Let's begin the meditation by taking a deep breath.

As you breathe in slowly through your nose and out your mouth, feel your chest and stomach rise and fall.

Now begin to notice your body.

Which parts of you are relaxed and which parts are tense?

Begin at your feet and examine your entire body.

Remember to tense and release any muscles that feel tight.

Relax your stomach and intestinal area.

Make sure your shoulders are down and relaxed.

Place your arms and hands in a natural position.

If necessary, adjust your body as you relax.

Now begin slowly counting to ten.

Next, take three deep breaths in through your nose and out your mouth.

Hold each breath for four seconds before you release it.

Release as much tension as you can and trust that your body will continue to relax naturally throughout the meditation.

Now visualize yourself standing in front of the gate you walked through in the last meditation.

Remember, you are the only one who can open the gate and travel to the places behind it.

Walk through the gate and close it.

Feel as if you are leaving all your concerns behind you on the other side of the gate.

Now begin walking along the familiar wooded pathway.

Notice the tall, strong trees and lush plant life as you walk forward.

Feel the ground beneath you and smell the richness of the soil.

Enjoy the beautiful sunny day.

Walk along until you begin to hear the stream in the distance.

Move quickly toward the stream.

When you are there, step off the path again onto the cool grass.

Sit down and take a moment to listen to the calming sounds of the water flowing over the rocks and the birds singing all around you.

Notice the colorful wildflowers and green ferns.

Take a deep breath and feel the peacefulness of this place.

Allow yourself to be completely in the moment, soaking up energy from the natural surroundings.

Take one last look at your surroundings

before you prepare to leave the stream and continue on your journey.

When you are ready, return to the pathway and begin walking again. Follow the path as it winds along beside the stream.

Look ahead and see a flower-covered meadow in the distance. Look beyond the clearing to see a tranquil lake.

Move closer to the lake and notice how perfectly still the water is.

Observe the color of the water and the types of trees that are growing along the shore.

Notice any wildlife such as fish, ducks, geese, or swans.

You may see other animals as well.

Now bend down and feel the coolness of

the water. Look into the water and see if you can make out your reflection.

Next, step back from the water and continue to explore the area until you find a comfortable place to sit.

Create a safe, comfortable environment that you will want to return to again and again.

Breathe in deeply until you feel a strong connection to the beauty of the lake.

Now begin to sense the presence of a loving light that's very near. Feel yourself become enveloped by this healing light.

Allow this Divine light to sweep through your body, uplifting and energizing you.

Fully experience the presence of the light.

Begin to think of a time in your life when you felt you were really loved.

Remember the experience deeply. Feel loved and accepted.

Notice how your body feels when you think about being loved.

Now think of a time when you were very loving and accepting of someone else.

How does your body feel when you are sending love?

Next, imagine that your love goes out in the form of a light. Visualize the color and shape of this light.

Now think of a person with whom you would like to share this light.

Choose the first person who comes to mind, no matter who it is.

You may even see the images of more than one person.

See this person or persons being surrounded by your loving light.

Continue to surround the person or persons until you feel they have absorbed as much of the light as possible.

Release their image and trust that the light will be used for their highest good.

Now take a moment to focus on yourself once more.

Begin to look out at the lake again and take a deep breath.

Take one last look at where you were sitting and prepare to leave.

Walk toward the pathway you followed earlier.

Make your way back past the stream to the tall trees.

When you see the gate, walk through it and close it behind you.

Know that you can bring these wonderful feelings of love back with you through the gate.

Take a deep breath and focus again on the room where you are meditating.

Notice how your muscles have relaxed during the meditation.

Continue with your day knowing you have experienced the gift of Divine love and have given it to someone else.

FOURTH MEDITATION

In this last meditation you will again take a walk along the pathway, reliving the relaxation, the perception of beauty, and the sense of Divine love experienced in the previous three meditations.

Then you will walk farther along the path until you reach the grandeur of a vast ocean. As you listen to the breaking surf, you will visualize certain events of your life and your sense of destiny and mission.

The purpose of this meditation is to use your skill of visualization to see particular directions in your life that will enhance your sense of love and service.

Meditation

Begin the meditation by taking a deep breath.

Breathe in and out slowly, expanding your chest and stomach.

Now begin to notice how your body is feeling today.

Begin with your feet and travel up your entire body.

Remember to tense and release any muscles that feel tight.

Make sure your shoulders are down and relaxed.

Feel your face soften.

Now count to ten slowly.

Take three deep breaths in through your nose and out your mouth.

Hold each breath for four seconds before you release it.

Feel your body becoming lighter with each breath.

Now survey your body again and adjust the way you are sitting or lying if you need to.

When you are ready, see yourself standing in front of the gate visualized in the earlier meditations.

Open the gate and walk through it.

As you close the gate, again feel as if you are leaving all your cares and concerns behind.

Now begin walking along the familiar pathway.

Don't forget to observe the trees and flowers that surround you.

Follow the pathway as it winds along beside the stream.

Stop for a moment and look at the water flowing over the rocks in the stream.

Now continue along the pathway until you see the lake in the distance. Instead of walking toward the lake, look to the right and see that there is another path that leads to a small hill.

Far in the distance behind the hill you

can see the horizon line of a vast, emerald-colored ocean.

As you walk toward the hill, begin to hear the waves rolling onto the shore.

Walk to the top of the hill and look out at the magnificent vista.

Proceed down the other side of the hill until you reach the sandy beach.

Notice the color of the sand and the water.

Breathe in the salty air.

Walk along in the sand for a moment and familiarize yourself with the environment.

When you are ready, sit down. You may want to sit directly in the sand or on a blanket or under a beach umbrella.

Look out at the water and closely observe the waves rolling onto the shore.

Feel a gentle breeze cooling your skin.

Begin to visualize the familiar light from the previous meditations.

Again feel the loving light sweep over your body, filling it with energy.

Breathe it in and feel it nourish every cell in your body.

Feel as if this Divine love knows you, understands you, and loves you deeply.

Now refocus your thoughts, remembering to keep this loving light within.

Let's now do a mental exercise similar to the one you did in the third meditation.

Think of something someone has done for you lately that you really appreciated.

It can be as simple as someone smiling at you in the elevator, or helping you fulfill an obligation.

Notice how your body feels as you recall the event.

Now think of something special that you could do for someone within the next twenty-four hours.

Your acts of kindness help add to others' experience of love, which amplifies, spreads, and makes the world a better place.

Now visualize a world where these acts are common and spontaneous, and where everyone is enveloped in love and sending it to others. How would the world shift? How would each person grow and evolve?

For a moment, think of your own life and of all the events that have happened to you since your birth.

Look closely for a consistent thread of meaning and destiny. What special contribution can you now make?

Ponder this question for as long as you wish. Then take a deep breath and notice that the sun is beginning to set and that it is time for you to return to the pathway.

Stand up and find the path you followed earlier.

Walk up the hill and stop to take one

last look at the ocean and the beauty of the horizon as the sun begins to set.

Continue on the path and begin to hear the stream in the distance.

Walk past the stream and make your way to the tall trees and the gate.

When you reach the gate, open it slowly and walk through.

Now become conscious of your physical body and move it around slowly.

Before you continue with your day, remember the journey you have taken and the insights that have come. Hold on to your intuitions and observe very closely.

Coincidences will occur as your deepest vision of yourself becomes real.